PLANNING OUTDOOR CHRISTIAN EDUCATION

An Administrative Guide
for Planners of Outdoor Experiences
with Older Elementary
Girls and Boys

by

Ronald K. Johnson

Published for The Cooperative Publication Association
by United Church Press   Philadelphia

This material has been developed through the cooperative effort of many denominations, seeking through an interdenominational agency, Cooperative Publication Association, to provide resources of the best quality.

Library of Congress Catalog Card Number 72-166400
ISBN 0-8298-0218-5

Table of Contents

INTRODUCTION

Christian education outdoors brings many images to mind—a sixth-grade class gathered around a charcoal grill behind their teacher's apartment house; day-campers lying on their backs in the shade of a towering elm in the city park; campers and their leaders hiking down a wooded trail to a secluded waterfall.

Not all of these experiences would normally be referred to as "camping." Neither would everything called camping be included under the heading of Christian education outdoors.

One thing is common to all these experiences—the outdoors. But each of them also involves learning, and each one has the potential of providing opportunity for Christian growth.

USING THE OUTDOORS

Wise teachers and leaders of older elementary girls and boys have always planned for informal, relaxed times to meet with their students apart from the regular classroom sessions. Outdoor education implies a change of pace, more time simply to be together, to think, to ask questions, and to discover answers in an unhurried way.

Recently a young mother stepped up to a middle-aged man at a church meeting. "Do you remember when you braided my hair each morning at camp?" she asked. Slowly a smile crept across the face of the former camp counselor as he thought back to those moments on the steps of a cabin by a lake twenty years before. He wondered if she still remembered from so long ago the probing questions that had poured from her lips as he brushed and then wove together the strands of her hair.

The main resource for learning in the outdoors is the outdoors itself. The mystery of birth and life, decay and death, is present everywhere outdoors. The interrelationship of all living things is waiting to be observed. Varieties of shape and size, of smell and taste, and of sounds and colors constantly challenge the senses. Beauty is found in the markings of a tiny caterpillar as well as in the twisted roots of a tree blown over by a storm. Curiosity is aroused, imagination is stimulated, and worship comes easily when persons are enjoying the outdoors.

The outdoors is also an exciting place to do things, to experience firsthand, to observe and explore. One group of boys and girls spent hours carefully inspecting a small patch of rock, weeds, and grass outside their church school classroom window. They identified more than twenty different grasses and plants, and several types of rock cropping out of two contrasting colors of soil. They compiled a long list of tiny insects, bugs, and worms, along with an inventory of bottles, cans, and trash—a sort of ecological disaster!

On a broader scale, other campers have observed the effects of climate, sun, and shade, and how plants and animals adapt to changing conditions. Basic questions about life—interrelationships, survival, adaptation— quite naturally follow exploration of the outdoors.

This administrative guide for planners of outdoor experiences with older elementary girls and boys is part of an outdoor Christian education series prepared for cooperative use by several denominations.

Church Camping by Robert Pickens Davis is the general administrative manual for sponsoring units, planning committees, and directors for all age levels. It should be referred to for information on budgets and record systems, the responsibilities of the planning committee and the director, job descriptions for various camp and outdoor education leaders, and help in the recruitment and training of outdoor education leaders.

Outdoor Living by LaDonna Bogardus is a guide for leaders of camping and other outdoor activities of the church for older elementary girls and boys.

Outdoor Living—Packet One includes poems, scripture references, and ideas and suggestions for discussion and worship; games, hymns, and songs. (Order 1 for each leader.)

Outdoor Living—Packet Two includes directions for developing a small camp, and for cooking, crafts, and other outdoor living activities. (Order several for each group.)

Outdoor Living—Packet Three includes twelve discovery guides for campers to use individually in exploring, experimenting, and thinking about meanings in specific areas. (Order 1 packet for each 2 or 3 campers.)

LEARNING OUTDOORS

Learning outdoors is not basically different or separate from learning in any other setting. Learning outdoors often presupposes previous learning experiences in the home and classroom and on the playground. Longer periods of discussion together as a group, as well as time alone to pursue personal interests and think and reflect, are often a part of outdoor education. A leisurely pace may offer opportunity to put together previously unrelated learnings. A less rigid schedule may include time to ask questions and come back again and again to a problem that is a special concern.

Persons learn in many ways. Outdoors there are often more opportunities to learn through the use of the senses—touching, testing, hearing, seeing, and smelling. Outdoors there are things to explore, experiments to try—and try again. Persons learn by trial and error and by thinking about their experiences. Persons learn by observing and finding answers. In these and many other ways girls and boys and their leaders learn some things best in the outdoors.

WHAT MAKES IT CHRISTIAN?

Outdoor education is properly referred to as *Christian* education when several conditions are fulfilled:

1. When outdoor experiences are related to ongoing experiences in other parts of the church's program.

2. When mature Christian leaders guide the activities and share their faith in God as creator.

3. When the purpose of the outdoor learning opportunities is the

Christian growth and understanding of the girls and boys and their leaders.

4. When questions about life and its meaning are welcomed and discussed freely in relationship to biblical teachings.

5. When worship is encouraged and openly expressed.

6. When love, acceptance, and concern for one another characterize the relationships between the girls and boys and their leaders.

Local church leaders are only beginning to take advantage of the many opportunities for learning outdoors. During a typical year the kindergarten class may have taken a walk to a nearby park and a few girls and boys may have registered for resident camp, but rarely have planning groups considered the possibility of *every* student sharing in Christian education outdoors.

A walk can become a ramble or a hike. Bicycles or other transportation make even more distant areas a possibility for outdoor experiences. City parks, church yards, farms, or public recreation areas near reservoirs, lakes, and rivers are often available for the asking. Of course, established campsites, whether owned by the local church, denomination, or a community group, are possibilities, along with state and national parks, forests, and recreation areas.

USING THE OUTDOORS AS A LEARNING ENVIRONMENT

Normally when we think of the outdoors we think only of traditional camp activities—cooking over a campfire, nature crafts, swimming, games, and other such activities. Yet the following list of ways of using the outdoors as a learning environment is only partial and suggestive:

Appreciation—of colors, forms, interrelationships, new discoveries

Enjoyment—of fresh air, cool nights, new sounds, a surprise snowfall, life itself

Observation—of variety in nature, habits of wildlife, stars at night

Perception—of tastes and smells, textures and hues, space and time

Reflection—on the meaning of life and growth, adaptation and change, death and decay

Worshiping—in response to the mystery and wonder of order, beauty, interrelatedness, interdependence

Investigation—of varieties in nature, adaptations to climate and environment, devastation resulting from man's misuse of the natural world

Discovery—of rare plants, unique rock formations, a hard-to-locate constellation

Developing—new skills, personal fitness, greater alertness

Creativity—encouraged by observing movement, design, and relationship in nature.

When you add several persons to the outdoor setting there will be opportunities for:

Fellowship—relaxed, informal, shared in a variety of activities

Associations—with new friends, with those of other ages, races, cultures

Participation—in new groupings, in eating new foods, in unfamiliar traditions

Cooperation—in solving problems, making decisions, achieving goals

Relationships—for longer periods of time, with persons having different life styles, or those known only superficially before

Discussion—about meanings, values, priorities, habits, decisions

Experimentation—with sharing, forgiving, understanding others

Action—especially in regard to pollution and ecological damage

CHARACTERISTICS OF CHRISTIAN EDUCATION OUTDOORS

There are several assumptions behind the many different opportunities listed above, assumptions that multiply the possibilities for learning and Christian growth in the outdoors.

One is _time_. Christian education outdoors almost takes for granted a more relaxed, extended experience than is usually scheduled for indoor activities. (Of course, shorter experiences outdoors also have value, as we shall see in chapter 4.) When we go outdoors we often spend several hours, most of a day, an overnight, several days, or even a week together. There is time for interpersonal relationships to grow and develop, time to express thoughts we were never quite ready to share in more limited times together. There is time to get to know the leaders and other persons in the group and to develop enough trust to risk questions that have been troubling for months or maybe years.

Too, we deal with _all of life_. Christian education outdoors involves everything that happens when the group is together. Fun times and serious times, work and play, cooperation and competition, discussion and worship, mealtime and rest time are all part of the agenda for teaching and learning in the outdoors.

There is a _relaxed informality_. A less hurried atmosphere seems natural in the outdoors. "Play" clothes signal freedom to sit or kneel or stretch out flat. First names and nicknames sound natural as friendships deepen. Sensitiveness to "girls' group" versus "boys' group" melts away before common interests in discovery and exploration. Time to just lie on your back and talk together with a friend may at first be derided as a nap, but soon is cherished as an opportunity for testing hopes and sharing hidden dreams.

A fourth assumption is a _focus on doing_. The reflection, worship, appreciation, and enjoyment mentioned above usually follow vigorous participation in some outdoor activity. A meal is cooked over a campfire. Class members take turns on a toboggan. A small group hikes to a nearby point of interest. Nature crafts challenge others in the group.

For some, repairing an eroded trail to the lake may bring new awareness of ecology and the interrelatedness of life.

Then there is the element of *fellowship*. The extent of individual sharing with others and the influence of the group on each of its members are both enlarged by the other characteristics of outdoor Christian education—more time, variety, informality, and activity. Fleeting Sunday morning acquaintances become lasting friends. The whole class is soon going arm in arm twelve abreast across the meadow, singing at the top of their voices! The strength gained from the experience of fellowship in the group reinforces individual decision and gives courage for lonely times in the future. Interracial and intercultural experiences come naturally when groups from many backgrounds are enjoying the outdoors together.

Yes, outdoor experiences are rich with possibilities for learning and Christian growth.

In his book *Church Camping*, Robert Davis defines church camping as "an experience in group living in an outdoor setting sponsored and directed by the church as a phase of its total educational program and under the supervision of mature Christian leadership. It utilizes the resources of the natural surroundings, interpersonal relationships, and the teachings of the Scriptures to contribute significantly to mental, physical, social, and spiritual growth." [1]

This definition suggests a particular content, program, and purpose for Christian education outdoors.

CONTENT

The content of outdoor education is the outdoors itself. Earth and sky, trees and flowers, birds and animals, water and sand—these are the resources for outdoor education. In most instances, the fewer man-made items you bring to the outdoor setting, the better. Or, to say it more positively, the greater your use of the natural environment in developing your program, the greater are the possiblities for meaningful outdoor education. Of course, a Bible and a limited number of resource books will usually be helpful, but you probably will not need a carload of artifical craft material.

[1] *Church Camping* by Robert Pickens Davis (Richmond: John Knox Press, 1969) p. 47.

In nature you will find grasses for weaving, bark and berries for coloring, and interesting shapes and textures for collages, mobiles, and other forms of self-expression. You can whittle many simple articles from pieces of wood. Designs in leaf and flower will inspire artistic expression. Struggling new plants in the midst of decay and death may stimulate discussions of the meaning of life and existence.

PROGRAM

If the content of outdoor education is the outdoors, the program may be described as "practicing Christian ways of living and relating to others" in that setting. A group of older elementary girls and boys experiencing firsthand the mystery and wonder, the struggle and violence of the world of nature, with time to talk about their experiences—this sums up the curriculum of outdoor education. One outdoor education book lists over three hundred "doing" kinds of activities that would challenge older elementary girls and boys as they explore together and try to understand the world around them and their place in it both as individuals and as a group.[1]

A program manual, camper activity packets, and other resource materials are available that suggest possible groupings of such activities into themes, areas, or discussion ideas, for those who desire to organize their outdoor experiences in that way.[2] But it is basically the needs and questions of the girls and boys, stimulated by the outdoor environment in which they are meeting, that provide the seemingly endless ideas of what to do.

PURPOSE

The purpose of Christian education outdoors is the same as the purpose of the entire program of the church—a growing awareness of God in Christ, and living out the meaning of that awareness in fellowship with God and with other persons in all of life. Christian education outdoors provides unique opportunities to experience the reality of God as creator, redeemer, healer, father, and as one who forgives and restores to fellowship. The longer hours together as a group provide an extended laboratory for trying out Christian living in an atmosphere of acceptance and trust. The outdoors invites experimentation with new ways of sharing with others and responding to them. There is time to try and fail and try again, with a group that stays together long enough to understand and accept both failure and success.

Now go back and read again the definition of church camping given in the first paragraph of this section. Do the phrases have more meaning? "An experience in group living in an outdoor setting," "utilizing the re-

---

[1] *Curriculum Enrichment Outdoors* by John W. Hug and Phyllis J. Wilson (New York: Harper and Row, 1965).

[2] *Outdoor Living:* A Guide for Camping and Other Outdoor Activities of the Church for Older Elementary Girls and Boys by LaDonna Bogardus (Nashville: Abingdon Press, 1970). Accompanying this guide are three packets, *Outdoor Living—Packets One, Two, and Three* (see page 6).

sources of the natural surroundings," "a phase of [the church's] total educational program." Do these words help you understand how the content, program, and purpose of Christian education outdoors interrelate and build on one another?

The outdoors is not always the best or even a better place for learning than other settings. But it does offer a unique opportunity for building upon the other learnings and in ways that may provide for dramatic growth in Christian living and understanding.

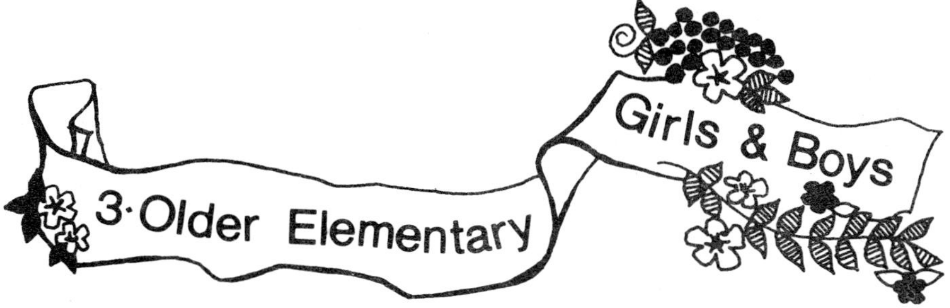

Outdoor Christian education implies active individual and group experiences and the use of fairly well developed skills in an outdoor setting. In terms of their physical and social growth and development ten- and eleven-year-olds are at a peak of readiness for active group use of their maturing abilities.

Older elementary girls and boys are ready for the less familiar outdoor environment. They can take care of all their personal physical needs without adult help. They have mastered the use of most simple tools, or are willing and eager to learn, and will work at developing any skills they have not had opportunity to gain previously. They are normally interested in a variety of activities, even though some girls and boys have already begun to develop special interests that take much of their time. Their physical coordination has developed to a point where there is less chance of injury in active exploration, play, or use of tools. They enjoy swimming or trying to learn.

Older elementary girls and boys are still in the gang stage and enjoy relatively brief associations in intimate groups or clubs, often with rules and codes that exclude others. A developing ability to organize and compete is combined with a natural tendency for teamwork and love for games. But sometimes the emphasis on rules and on what is right means that they spend ten minutes playing ball and twenty minutes arguing some fine point of the rules of the game! Girls and boys still have comparable endurance and skills, a fact that the boys must often reluctantly admit when the girls beat them at some physical activity.

At one resident camp the boys resented the girls in the group until one evening when they were all carrying their sleeping bags across a small ravine to a clearing on the opposite hill. The boys, as usual, had hurried ahead. Half way up the far side of the ravine the boys stopped to rest, for the sleeping bags were quite a load. While they waited, along came the girls. But instead of stopping to rest, the girls quickly picked up the boys' sleeping bags along with their own and continued on up the hill. Suddenly the boys decided it was not too tragic to have girls in their group!

These girls and boys are curious about how things are made, how each part takes its place in an interdependent cycle in nature. They are almost constantly on the go. Adults need to provide—even insist on—periods of rest and inactivity. And not every moment is best spent in the group. Most older boys and girls need some time alone, some privacy for personal thoughts and self-evaluation. There is a place for secrets; and confidences shared with adults must always be honored if we respect the growing child's developing awareness of himself as a unique individual.

Sex differences are most evident in the teaming up of boys against girls. There may even be some antagonism between sexes. But usually there is only the banter back and forth that is an outward sign of the struggle to know what it means to be a preadolescent girl or boy. The best evidence that sex differences are only lightly held is the relative ease with which girls and boys work together naturally on almost any project in which they have a personal interest. Making plaster casts of fresh animal tracks suddenly becomes a mutual project for boys and girls, though only moments before they were teasing one another mercilessly. Some of the older girls will have begun menstruation and some may be self-conscious about their developing bodies.

Television and modern educational methods have accelerated their intellectual growth and awareness to a degree never before known for ten- and eleven-year-olds. The image many adults have of what to expect of older girls and boys is far out of date. These children are not only aware of what is going on all around the world, but also can spout facts about the universe that were not even discovered when the adults were in school! Many of them have had experience in working in committees and small groups, organizing material, and reporting in summary form. The great majority are trained to use the problem-solving approach, and they quite naturally see that most questions have at least two sides. They are interested in the ideas of others, and can evaluate their own contributions to a group. Imagine the possibilities for learning and Christian growth in the outdoors with such girls and boys!

Christian education outdoors is built around meaningful group use of resources found in the natural environment. Many persons think of going to some far-off campsite in the woods when they think of using the outdoors with older girls and boys. Outdoor education, as used by the church, is a much broader concept. Many different settings or locations may be found useful, depending on the purpose for choosing the outdoors for certain parts of the program of Christian education.

A NATURAL SETTING

The primary requirement for an outdoor learning experience is the outdoors! This may mean the lawn and flower bed just outside the door to the church school classroom. It might include a nearby city park, a class member's back yard, a friend's farm, or a campsite specifically planned for Christian outdoor education. As the particular purpose for an outdoor experience with boys and girls is planned, it may be felt that a place with trees or wildlife or rocks is needed. But the first step is to plan for the use of the outdoors itself for learning.

A SETTING THAT OFFERS VARIETY

Opportunities for learning are usually multiplied by the variety present in any particular setting. The more kinds of trees and flowers, rocks and minerals, animals and birds, the better. And do not leave out creepy and crawly things! One particular color or shape may be intriguing to one person or group but may have no meaning to others. The thing that challenges the rest of the group may be learning about unique rock formations nearby and what they reveal of the geological history of the area.

Variety may be where you least expect to find it. There are mystery and beauty in a sand dune that will challenge almost any group. What may seem to be endless grains of sand to some will be a symphony of movement, form, and shading to others. And the thrill of discovering a tiny plant or small bug in the midst of all that sand is matched by the almost immediate questions of how and why it can exist in such a hostile environment.

Nor does variety imply miles and miles of countryside. Some boys and girls have learned about the wonder and mystery of God's world by carefully examining the first few inches of top soil in one square foot of earth. Elaborate root systems, bits of refuse in varying stages of decay, shadings of color, variations in moisture, tiny animals that are barely visible even through a magnifying glass—all these speak of God's plan for life and death, for interrelatedness, for adaptation to environment.

If your purpose includes nature crafts, the site should have a plentiful supply of whatever is needed—bark, shells, moss, grass, twigs—enough so that future groups will find ample resources for their own use.

The need for variety in the environment is also related to the length of time a group plans to use a site. A rather limited number of unique features will provide the resources for a one-day learning experience. A much greater variety of natural resources would be desired for a day camp lasting more than a week.

A PLACE TO EXPLORE

We have noted that older elementary girls and boys are normally busy and active and often learn best by experiencing for themselves what we so often try to teach by "telling." A place for outdoor learning experiences probably should include maximum opportunity for exploration and for participation in a variety of activities. The thrill of discovery is as real today as it ever was. These older girls and boys may someday be investigating some unexplored lunar crater. But for now there is almost as much excitement and reward in discovering the first blackberries of the season, a four-leaf clover, the track of a deer in moist earth, or a fossil in a rock that everyone else had walked right by!

The outdoor setting that is chosen should have a place to cook a meal over a small campfire, using wood that has been gathered in the vicinity and food that the girls and boys have prepared themselves. For places where fire regulations prohibit open fires, small portable charcoal stoves are now available for hikers to carry along.

Exploration does not necessarily mean vast distances. Hikes with older girls and boys might better be called walks or rambles, since they are usually of shorter duration and are planned for other purposes than simply covering many miles. Ten- and eleven-year-olds should stick to well-defined trails or old roadways when hiking. There are many advantages when the group stays together on the trail. Those with more energy and strength may feel held back at first, but they soon find greater satisfaction in being with the slower ones and helping by carrying their packs. When all members of the group are in sight of one another, the discovery of a rare flower or a hummingbird's nest can be shared with the whole group. Singing along the trail may be the cementing factor for a group that until that moment had not quite found itself.

It would be unusual for one outdoor site to offer all the opportunities to explore that might be desired during a year. Planning groups and leaders often choose one place for snow activities in winter and a different location for water activities in summer. One site may offer evidences of erosion or pollution that would tie in with the purpose of a particular learning experience. Some places are best for discovering evidence of the geological history of an area. In some areas several life cycles involving plants, animals, and soil are easily observed, while another area may have greater variety of certain kinds of plant or animal life. Sometimes a place is wanted where food and shelter are provided and maximum time can be spent in group discussion, deepening fellowship, and trying new ways of relating together as a group. Another time the same goals might be sought as the group works together in building their own simple shelters and sanitary facilities.

The purpose or goal for a particular outdoor learning experience will largely determine the kind and type of setting chosen.

NEED FOR PRIVACY

What has been said so far about the setting implies a certain amount of privacy. There can be a variety of things to do and explore on a site, but if dozens of other persons are walking through the same area or sitting at the next picnic table it is difficult to meet all the needs that led to the choice of that particular outdoor setting. Loud talking or shouting from groups on nearby property, bothersome traffic sounds from adjacent roads, or distracting activity in full view of the boys and girls all tend to frustrate learning possibilities.

When choosing a place for groups to meet outdoors such possible outside interference should be considered. Often, by choosing a different day of the week or even a different time of day, such distractions can be minimized or even avoided. For instance a city park may be crowded on weekends and weekday afternoons, but be almost deserted weekday mornings.

Individual ten- and eleven-year-old girls and boys also need an opportunity to be by themselves once in a while. An outdoor meeting place that does not provide a single place where one may sit for a while out of sight of everyone else may not be the best site for an extended outdoor learning experience. The boys and girls at one campsite discovered that what looked like an old trail came to an end at a small log only a short distance off the main trail. They agreed to save that log for anyone who wanted to be alone for a while. They fixed a signal at the main trail to indicate that someone was using the spot. Every day several of the girls and boys chose that place to think through difficult decisions, to meditate and pray, or to regain their composure after some hurt or argument.

Finding a place away from people, noise, and distractions may become more and more difficult as our population expands and cities move to the suburbs and the suburbs take over farmland and forest. If compromises need to be made between privacy and available sites, let the choice be made while thinking carefully about the purpose of the particular outdoor learning experience and the needs of ten- and eleven-year-old girls and boys.

NEED FOR BUILDINGS AND FACILITIES

There is no one set of requirements for buildings and equipment needed for Christian outdoor education. With a variety of possible outdoor activities planned for varying lengths of time and located different distances from the homes of the girls and boys, the physical facilities needed on a chosen site may vary from none to complete housing, sanitary, and eating facilities.

Toilet facilities may already be available nearby if the outdoor site is in a city or state park or near a church, home, or farm. For a day camp or hike, sack lunches and drinking water can be carried along each day. Sleeping bags with plastic ground cloths and covers will suffice for an occasional overnight experience.

Day camp sites should have, as a minimum, a drinking water supply, toilet facilities that meet local health requirements, a central shelter for inclement weather, and a storage place for equipment and supplies.

Resident camp facilities also need kitchen and dining facilities, tents or cabins for sleeping, and arrangements for disposal of garbage and other waste materials. Shower facilities are usually provided.

Christian education outdoors de-emphasizes the need for physical facilities on the site and maximizes the use of the outdoor setting itself. Once health and safety requirements have been met, most leaders prefer a minimum of buildings and civilized comforts, so that every opportunity is taken to utilize the resources of that particular site in their program of Christian education outdoors.

Ten- and eleven-year-olds enjoy cooking their own meals, but are not yet able to prepare three meals a day and still have much time left over for any other activity. Consequently it is usually recommended that one or two meals a day be provided for them. There have been successful rustic camping experiences with boys and girls this age who have had training ahead of time and who enjoy the luxury of highly skilled leaders. Day camping may be the best choice for a typical local church group of ten- and eleven-year-olds. They stay at home each night, and can bring their own sack lunches or food for a cookout in the middle of the day. Drinking water can be hauled each day to a campsite if necessary. Temporary toilet facilities may be rented or, if local health codes allow, provided in the form of pit latrines. Costs are minimal and class groups can often attend together with their regular teachers and leaders, supplemented by persons more familiar with outdoor activities.

SAFETY OF THE CAMPERS

What do you do if the "ideal" outdoor education site is covered with poison ivy? Would you choose a site with several vertical cliffs on the property? Maybe there are old open mine shafts in the nearby woods. Should chiggers and mosquitoes deter you from choosing a particular location?

Obviously the safety of the boys and girls using the site must be kept in mind. Such hazards as poisonous plants and reptiles, steep cliffs and riverbanks, and other dangers to life and limb should be identified ahead of any outdoor education experience. Action must then be taken to either make the dangerous areas "out of bounds" or warn campers about them and be prepared to handle possible emergencies. It may be better to choose another site. On the other hand, adults may be too protective. Older boys and girls have good sense and should be expected to use it. Most activities should involve the group, and group decisions will avoid most serious dangers.

The success of outdoor Christian education rests largely with those persons designated as leaders. A planning committee may think of every detail, the outdoor setting may offer tremendous possibilities, the boys and girls may be eager and excited, but without mature Christian leadership the entire experience may be a failure. The leaders must relate the outdoor experience to the continuing program of education in the church. The leaders are often needed to suggest how outdoor resources might be used to promote Christian growth and understanding. The leaders can help each individual struggle with his own questions about meanings and relationships.

A GROWING CHRISTIAN

First of all, the leader of an outdoor Christian education experience needs to be reasonably mature, yet growing in his understanding and experience of the Christian faith. Outdoor experiences tend to raise concerns about feelings and meanings, rather than questions about factual detail. The leader should have already faced the meaning of life and death. He should have grappled deeply with the problem of suffering and evil. His understanding of the teachings of Jesus should enable him to help boys and girls think deeply about such basic concerns as God's love, forgiveness, and what it means to "turn the other cheek." The leader's faith will be more evident in his ways of dealing with others than in his words. He will find that much of the "teaching" will be done through his immediate responses to unexpected questions throughout the day. A good leader is one who lives his faith hour by hour and who is occasionally willing to say, "*I* wonder about that, too. What do *you* think?"

A FRIEND OF BOYS AND GIRLS

An effective leader understands and loves girls and boys. He is aware of the struggles each one is going through to discover who he is as an individual, as a preadolescent, and as a maturing Christian. He loves the fresh openness and active enthusiasm of the girls and boys. He understands when they need to be alone for a time. He encourages them when they want so much to have friends, but hold back. He is a patient teacher when they work on improving their skills by doing a task over and over again. He recognizes when he must gently but firmly require a rest hour during the day, for he knows they are often stimulated by the group beyond their normal endurance and strength. The effective leader is interested in the ideas of the girls and boys, he laughs at their ancient jokes (new to them), and he dreams with them of what life as an adult might be.

RELAXED IN THE OUTDOORS

Christian education outdoors requires leaders that are at ease sitting under a tree, sleeping in a tent, or examining the frog a camper has captured. Cooking over an open fire is obviously fun for them. Not that every leader is a skilled outdoorsman. Rather he is appreciative of the beauty and variety in nature and is willing to learn even more about it along with the boys and girls. Many leaders have acquired their love of nature from childhood experiences with their families. Others have learned the joys of the outdoors from outdoor experiences in church camps or camps sponsored by the "Y," Scouts, or Camp Fire Girl groups.

Leaders trained for guiding outdoor experiences are not always available. It is then the responsibility of the planning committee to provide opportunities for other leaders to spend some time learning the skills of outdoor living before they attempt experiences with girls and boys. It is amazing how one or two meals cooked over a campfire, a hike along a trail that the campers might be taking later, and a few hours of practicing skills together will bring confidence and poise to a group of previously untrained leaders.

AND EVEN MORE

In addition to Christian maturity, knowledge of what older girls and boys are like, and a love of the outdoors, there are other things to look for when recruiting leaders for outdoor education in the church.

Flexibility is important and is one of the earmarks of outdoor education. Plans are not followed rigidly. A discovery along the trail, an emerging need expressed by a camper, a sudden change in the weather —and plans must be modified or completely changed.

A good leader is observant in the outdoors. Being aware of a tired camper, pointing out a beautiful sunset, or helping discover fresh animal tracks nearby, all add to the enjoyment and meaning of outdoor experiences.

Imagination and creativity also add enrichment to outdoor activities. A piece of driftwood becomes an animal pin. Tall grasses are woven into place mats. Delicate vein patterns on a leaf are transformed into distinctive note paper, using a green ink pad. A never-ending variety of sights, sounds, colors, and shapes will provide the creative person with all the "activities" needed to challenge ten- and eleven-year-olds.

One minister remarked, when hearing the suggested list of characteristics of a leader of outdoor Christian education, "Wow! If there is even one mature, growing Christian in my church, who also loves girls and boys and understands their ways, who is at home in the outdoors, and furthermore is creative, flexible, and observant—I'd like to know about that person. I could use him in a dozen places in the ministry of the church!"

There may not be any ideal leaders for outdoor experiences. But a good leader can encourage Christian growth and awareness of God even when the setting has many drawbacks, when it rains every day, or all the girls and boys appear to have problems. But it doesn't work the other way around. Even with a perfect campsite, eager campers will be denied most opportunities for maturing in relationships with others and with God if the leaders are themselves immature, tense, and lacking in understanding.

The message is clear. Find trained leaders, or train the leaders you have, so the girls and boys in your church can enjoy Christian education outdoors.[1]

Many possibilities for outdoor educational experiences have already been mentioned, especially in chapter 4. In the pages that follow, these activities are listed by category, along with some additional suggestions for planning groups in local churches. Planning committees may think of other possibilities or at least variations of the suggestions given.

1. *Regular Sunday or weekday class sessions may be held outdoors* for all or part of a period:

(a) when the theme being studied is God's World, Stewardship of Natural Resources, or a similar topic. *Purpose:* to observe at firsthand objects outdoors that are related to the subject being studied in class, noting possible outdoor activities that would involve class members.

(b) when the theme being studied is in the area of Friends, Sharing in the Community, or Being Human Together. *Purpose:* to practice new ways of relating to one another as Christians while participating in activities together outdoors.

(c) when an activity in the community is a natural part of the progression of classroom studies. *Purpose:* to follow through on a group decision to carry out some project in the community.

2. *Additional weekday class sessions may be held outdoors:*

(a) when the length of regular Sunday or weekday class sessions is not sufficient to carry out an activity planned for outdoors. *Purpose:* to provide a longer period of time to complete a planned outdoor activity.

(b) when some or all of the older elementary boys and girls in a group are interested in a project for which an outdoor setting is needed. *Purpose:* to provide outdoor experiences for those class members who are interested in a particular outdoor project such as cleaning up broken glass and other hazards near an outdoor play area for younger children.

(c) when there is need for a variety of class activities, including social and recreational events outdoors. *Purpose:* to provide an opportunity for

---

[1] For further information about recruiting and training leaders, see *Church Camping* by Robert Pickens Davis, especially pages 65-90.

leaders and class members to be together in a more relaxed, outdoor setting.

(d) when leaders of an older elementary class need to have additional time for getting to know one another and developing "groupness." *Purpose:* to provide experiences outdoors that give maximum opportunity to group members to practice skills in working together with one another and with the group.

3. *Weekday sessions for new groupings of boys and girls may be held:*

(a) whenever interest is expressed in outdoor activities such as hikes, cookouts, explorations, snow trips, or water-related activities such as swimming, boating, collecting driftwood or shells. *Purpose:* to provide opportunities for those interested in particular outdoor activities under church leadership.

4. *Day camp experiences may be provided:*
   (a) sponsored by
      —a single local church
      —several local churches of the same denomination
      —an ecumenical grouping of churches
      —a coalition of church and community agencies such as Scouts, 4-H, Lions, women's clubs
   (b) planned for boys and girls from
      —the same grade or class in school
      —any older elementary class in a church
      —several local churches
      —several different racial and cultural backgrounds
   (c) scheduled for
      —morning and afternoon each day
      —afternoon and evening each day
      —several days with one overnight
      —one five-day week
      —two five-day weeks
      —almost any other variation that provides at least three consecutive days the first week

5. *Resident camps may be provided:*
   (a) sponsored by
      —one local church
      —several local churches in an area
      —area or regional camp committees or associations of local churches
      —coalition groups of church and community agencies
   (b) planned for
      —older elementary children who are either entering or completing the fifth or sixth grade in churches of one denomination
      —boys and girls from a variety of racial, cultural, and denominational backgrounds

(c) scheduled for
—a minimum of five days
—ten days or two weeks, when adequate leadership is available [1]

Christian education outdoors includes many different kinds of experiences lasting for varying periods of time. Thus no hard and fast rules for sizes of groups can be given. Leaders have discovered from experience, however, that there are some limits that should be exceeded only after careful thought and preparation. The sections that follow include some general recommendations.

When organized classes meet outdoors for one or more sessions the grouping is whatever size the class happens to be. If the regular teachers are prepared to lead the outdoor activities, no additional leaders may be needed. But often it is helpful to add one or more leaders with special skills in the subject area chosen as the theme of the outdoor session. If there are more than six students for each leader, an effort probably should be made to find additional adults so that more individual attention can be given to each student. Even if all the regular leaders are uneasy in an outdoor setting, it is helpful if at least one of them can join the class outdoors in order to provide continuity with previous class work and security for students who may be equally uneasy outdoors.

Three or four students may work together in discovering and comparing evidences of adaptation to climate and environment. Individuals may work alone in painting scenes with colors they obtain from flowers, berries, leaves, rocks, and bark. The entire class may be together to talk about meanings and relationships they have experienced. Greater variety in grouping is possible because the class members are already acquainted with one another and with their leaders.

When groups of older elementary boys and girls from one local church meet for outdoor sessions some of the same dynamics are present. The students may already know one another and the leaders. If there are more than eight or ten students it may be best to divide them into two

---

[1] Additional information about staff, job descriptions, budget, necessary forms and blanks for day, resident, and family camping may be found in *Church Camping* by Robert Pickens Davis.

small groups, each with a leader. It would normally be best to divide according to age, though there will be times when girls and boys would rather be in separate small groups. But at other times intense interest in particular projects will take preference over age and sex groupings.

If those choosing an outdoor activity are from different class groups, more time will need to be spent in getting to know one another, setting goals as individuals and as a group, and deciding on a plan for working toward each goal.

It is helpful if there can be an adult for every four or five fifth- and sixth-graders so they will have adequate guidance as they work through their questions and problems. After the members of each small group have learned to work together there will be less need for the adults, but they will "be around" when the students want to check something with them.

When older elementary boys and girls participate in a day camp it is usually best to have an adult with each four to six campers. More mature sixth-graders may form larger groupings, especially if the leaders are experienced and some of the campers have attended a day camp before.

It is recommended that most activities be organized with groups including two adults and eight to ten campers. Half might be boys and half girls. Two leaders make possible more individual attention, when it is desired, and offer a greater variety of skills and resources to the group. Many times the campers express an interest in an area with which one of the adults is totally unfamiliar. Hopefully, the other adult may be able to help out at that point, or the group might "borrow" a leader from another small group for a brief period.

Two leaders are usually needed when the group leaves the central day camp area. One leader can be with the more active group that always seems to push ahead. The second leader can be sure that the slower ones are urged along and that no one is left behind.

The small group of eight or ten may plan and carry out most of the activities during the day in camp—making a shelter, cooking, resting, planning, singing, exploring—especially the first day or two, when the boys and girls are learning to work together as a group. After several days, small groups may be ready to join others in carrying out certain projects, or to share their discoveries with other small groups or possibly with the entire camp. Fifth-graders may be satisfied to remain in their small group throughout the entire day camp. Older sixth-graders are more likely to want to spend some time with other small groups of campers their own age.

Day camps may include as many as sixty campers in the total group, and even more, if the site is large enough so that small groups may spend most of their time by themselves.

When fifth- and sixth-graders attend a resident camp they are likely to be with campers from many other local churches. Even if there are several boys and girls from each local church at the camp, an effort should be made to group campers so that they will be with *some* persons they already know and still have the opportunity to make some *new* friends in their small group.

As with day camping, it is usually recommended that two adults and eight to ten campers form the basic small groups for most activities. It is helpful if each adult and his four or five campers can be housed in a separate shelter. Two temporary canvas shelters or tents, two opposite ends of a divided cabin, or two groups of beds separated by empty beds in dormitory-style housing, all have been used successfully to provide a place of their own for each group of five or six.

It is much more practical for the girls and the boys to live nearby than to be separated on opposite sides of the campsite. Since most of their activities will be done together as a small group, informal planning and sharing can continue on the steps of the girls' cabin if the two shelters are side by side.

Camp directors have experimented with camps of many different sizes. In camps of not over forty or fifty-campers there is obviously less confusion and rushing around, there are fewer discipline problems, and it is easier to establish and maintain a relaxed atmosphere. But a larger camp, with typical volunteer leadership, begins to experience difficulties with extremes of behavior, tiredness even with normal rest hours, and a certain amount of tension simply from being in such a large group, especially at mealtimes.

Some camp directors, blessed with experienced, trained leaders, and a large campsite, have camped sucessfully with larger groups. There is usually pressure from camp managers to enroll 100 or more campers, and some state park group campsites penalize camps with less than 150! If the economics of operating a campsite call for that many campers your group might share the site with another group. If the site allows reasonable privacy for each group, sharing a large campsite may be a better solution than enrolling more than sixty older elementary boys and girls in one resident camp.

For years preschool leaders have sent home permission slips for parents to sign, giving their consent for their children to go on a field trip, a walk to a nearby park, or to participate in some other outdoor activity. There may be situations when parental permission will be needed even for older elementary boys and girls. At least the parents should know where their children are at any given time.

Other matters of health and safety should also be considered.

INSURANCE

Many churches carry accident insurance on persons using the church building and adjacent church property. You may need to check to see if students are protected if they go somewhere away from the church building. Low-cost accident insurance is often available from denominational state, or regional offices for one or more days, a week, or even longer periods of time.

FIRST AID

A small pocket first-aid kit may give a greater sense of security than actual protection, but it is amazing what a Band-Aid over a cut or bruise does to injured feelings. The new antiseptic solutions do help control infection that might otherwise get a start in a scratch or a broken blister.

The staff of every day camp and resident camp should include an advanced first aider or a nurse. Advance arrangements should be made with a doctor and a hospital for emergency assistance if it is needed. Emergency transportation should always be available. Camp leaders are often lulled into complacency when there are no injuries requiring medical attention over a period of several years. As a minimum, the counselor with the most first-aid training should be designated as health counselor and be available for consultation after each meal. A bit of personal attention and someone to talk to often wards off what might turn into a serious case of homesickness, an upset stomach, or a mean headache.

MEDICATIONS

It is amazing how many pills people take these days! And some of them are very important. With these medications many boys and girls are able to participate normally in society. A few years ago such children would have been dropouts. It is important that information about needed medications be solicited from parents in advance so that leaders can make sure that campers follow their doctor's directions.

DRINKING WATER

Because of pollution from an expanding population there remain few springs or mountain streams that are pure enough for drinking. Hikers should carry canteens and fill them from tested water supplies. In an emergency, tablets are available that will purify water for drinking, but they leave an undesirable taste in the water.

Day camp and resident camp sites must have a supply of pure water available; otherwise water must be hauled to the site each day.

TOILET FACILITIES

Nearly all county and township units now have strict health standards, even for what are usually considered rural areas. If local health rules permit, pit latrines may be used for short outdoor activities or day camps. But it is usually more satisfactory and more sanitary to rent a portable chemical toilet for the duration of the camp. Resident campsites should meet American Camping Association health standards which require a certain number of toilets and showers in proportion to the number of campers using the site.

GARBAGE

All but the most remote campsites need to make arrangements for garbage disposal. Renewed interest in control of pollution and protection of the environment has made past disposal practices obsolete. Each small group taking sack lunches on a hike, or cooking out, should return all trash and leftovers to the garbage cans in the center of the campsite.

WATERFRONT

A trained lifeguard or waterfront safety instructor should be in charge of every group that goes swimming. (Check local and state laws about waterfront supervision.) A lifeguard not only protects the safety of the campers but may also help to make their time in the water more enjoyable. There may be time for swimming lessons. Water games may involve both swimmers and nonswimmers.

POISONOUS PLANTS AND INSECTS

Familiarity may be the best prevention if the campsite has poison ivy or other poisonous plants near paths or buildings. Be sure each camper can identify the leaves and is aware of areas where the plants are most abundant.

When boys and girls are exposed to mosquitoes, gnats, bees, and other such insects, insect repellent and lotion to relieve the itch from bites and stings should be on hand. Usually some immunity builds up in time, but some campers need all the sympathy and calamine lotion you can give them! Be aware of any bee and wasp sting allergies noted on campers' health cards, and have on hand any medication that may be specified for treatment.

REST TIME

Time for rest and sleep is always the subject of a struggle between campers and leaders. Boys and girls do not realize that when they are home they pace themselves and take short rests all during the day. At camp there is a tendency to keep going without a break all day. The typical daily schedule for day camps and resident camps calls for an hour or so of "flat time" after lunch. Normally, after a few days the boys and girls are looking forward to this opportunity to read, write letters, rest, or even sleep.[1]

---

[1] *Church Camping* by Robert Pickens Davis has additional information about camp health and safety, including health, sanitation, and safety forms and records in an Appendix, pp. 104-31.

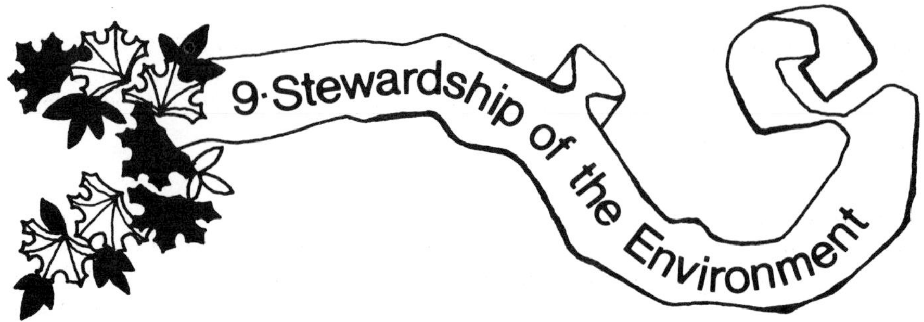

Ecology—the study of the relationship of the interdependency between organisms and their environment—was an almost unknown word when John Storer wrote *The Web of Life* in 1953. Now it is a word used every day in the newspapers, on television, and whenever people talk about life together as humans. Christian education outdoors involves doing things in the natural environment. Such activity could mean disruption and even destruction of things in nature. Or it could mean greater awareness of the interdependence, order, and beauty in nature.

LIVING OUTDOORS

The first rule of outdoor living might be: "Before you leave an area, restore it as nearly as possible to the condition in which you found it." Lashings and other construction should be taken down so the next group can "discover" the same natural spot that the previous group enjoyed. Some groups have even replaced twigs and branches they had cleared from grassy spots where they slept at night.

A second rule might be: Leave the site in *better* condition than you found it! A trail might be re-routed if the present location is causing serious erosion problems. Erosion damage could be repaired, and trees planted and watered (to be sure they will live).

A third rule is implied in the first two: Enjoy the outdoors; investigate its surprising variety and order; observe its colors, shapes, formations; explore its hidden wonders; discover its rare plants, interesting tastes and smells—but leave it all there for others to enjoy, investigate, observe, explore, and discover.

A fourth rule is: Don't litter! A gum wrapper along the trail, an aluminum can in a waterfall, a Styrofoam cup among the wildflowers, discarded plastic sacks in a high mountain meadow—each item was "the only thing" one camper left behind. But such carelessness on the part of hundreds of campers over a single summer can turn a beautiful area into a dump.

Some groups have planned hikes with the special purpose of picking up litter and carrying it to garbage disposal stations.

KEEPING IT LIKE IT IS

Various ideas have been tried in order to keep an outdoor area as nearly as possible in its natural state and still permit outdoor experiences on portions of the site.

One plan is to limit persons to specific activity sites and to marked trails that circle throughout much of the remaining area. Even when heavily traveled trails have to be specially surfaced because of hard use, areas adjacent to the trails can be kept almost untouched.

Another arrangement is to set aside special areas for different activities. All cutting of trees, sawing, and chopping is done in one area. Fires and cookouts are limited to another area. Special nature trails are maintained through the areas with the greatest variety of plant life. Other more primitive areas are available for exploration off the trail.

Christian education outdoors might include girls and boys and their leaders taking active roles in protecting, renewing, and preserving the outdoors. Nine- and ten-year olds might write letters and visit public officials to call attention to misuse of natural areas. They could plant trees and shrubs and help restore eroded or overused areas. Participation in action projects that help clean up, renew, or protect the natural environment may be one way to help older elementary girls and boys grow in their understanding of the mission of the church.

Such projects can be part of "an experience in group living in an outdoor setting," "utilizing the resources of the natural surroundings," and "a phase of [the church's] total educational program"—Christian education outdoors!

RESOURCES

Unless otherwise indicated, the following books may be secured from your denominational bookstores.

ADMINISTRATION OF CHURCH CAMPING

Church Camping by Robert Pickens Davis (Richmond: John Knox Press, 1969) Paper, $3.25. An administrative manual that deals with church-sponsored experiences in group living which utilize natural resources. Serves all phases of church camping by giving help to sponsoring unit, planning committee, and camp director.

Growing Inside, Outside by Bud Harper (Toronto: The United Church Publishing House, The United Church of Canada, 1969) $1.50. A manual that considers the purpose and planning necessary for Christian experiences outdoors.

PHILOSOPHY OF OUTDOOR EDUCATION

Outdoor Education: Principles and Practice by Cecil Garrison (Springfield, Ill.: Charles C. Thomas, 1966) $9.50. Both the *how* and *why* of outdoor activities are stressed in this guide for leaders, written expressly as a college text for classes in outdoor education. *Outdoor Education: A Book of Readings* by Donald R. Hammerman and William H. Hammerman (Minneapolis: Burgess Publishing Company, 1968) $7.50. A summary of practices and principles in outdoor education.

LEARNING OUTDOORS WITH BOYS AND GIRLS

Classroom Out-of-Doors: Education Through School Camping by Wilbur Lang Schramm. (Kalamazoo: Sequoia Press, 1969) $4.95. Curiosity and discovery are recurring words in this book which describes *how* as well as *what* sixth-grade children learn in a public school camp.

Field Study Manual for Outdoor Learning by Margaret Milliken, et. al. (Minneapolis: Burgess Publishing Company, 1968) Spiral binding, $2.95. Written for outdoor use with boys and girls in grades 5-8.

Outdoor Education by Charles L. Mand (New York: J. Lowell Pratt & Co., 1967) Paper, $2.95. A teacher's guide to relating children to the outdoors.

Between Parent and Child by Haim G. Ginott (New York: Avon Books, 1969) Paper, $1.25. A book on communication, designed to establish a relationship of mutual responsibility, love, and respect.

Let's Play by LaDonna Bogardus (New York: National Council of Churches, 1958) Paper, 70 cents. Guide for play activities outdoors with six-to-twelve-year-olds.

Let's Teach Through Group Relations by Dorothy W. Caton (New York: National Council of Churches, 1959) Paper, $1.00. For leaders of six-to-twelve-year-olds to guide in using group activities outdoors.

Let's Go Exploring by Leo Rippy, Jr. (New York: National Council of Churches, 1959) Paper, 60 cents. Guidance for leaders in outdoor activities with the six-to-twelve-year-olds. Useful in training leaders.

CAMPSITE DEVELOPMENT AND MANAGEMENT

Site Selection and Development: Camps, Conferences, Retreats by Bone, Britten, Brown, Davis, and Schlingman. (Philadelphia: United Church Press, 1965) $12.50. Comprehensive and authoritative guide on master planning, factors in site selection, land use and management, facilities, administration and finances.

Camp Site Development by Julian H. Salomon (Girl Scouts of the U.S.A., 1959). Order from nearest Girl Scout Equipment Agency. Catalog 19-527. Paper, $3.00. Covers all aspects from choice of site to design of buildings.

Campsites and Facilities (Boy Scouts of America, New Brunswick, New Jersey, 1950) $7.50. Discussion of the many factors involved in the selection and development of camp facilities.

Swimming Pool Management by Charles C. Stott (Management Aids Bulletin No. 49, National Recreation and Park Association, 1700 Pennsylvania Avenue, N. W., Washington, D. C. 20006, 1965) Members, $1.00; non-members, $2.00. A manual on personnel, training, and safety.

LEADERS AND COUNSELORS

Cues for Church Camping, for Counselors of Juniors and Junior Highs. Board of Christian Education, United Presbyterian Church. (Philadelphia: Geneva Press, 1962) Paper, $1.00. A guide to assist the counselor in interpreting the spiritual values inherent in camping.

Training Camp Counselors in Human Relations by Jerry Beker (New York: Association Press, 1962) $3.75. Forty-two case histories useful for training counselors to deal with tension-building situations in camp.

Leading a Group: A Guide for Your Preparation by Dorothy LaCroix Hill (735-BC). (Nashville: General Board of Education of The Methodist Church, 1966) Paper, 50 cents. Basic guidance in group work, designed for use by Christian education leaders.

KINDS OF OUTDOOR EDUCATION ACTIVITIES

So You Want to Start a Day Camp. American Camping Association, Inc., 1964. Paper, $1.25. Basic essentials of planning and administering a day camp.

The Day Camp Program Book by Virginia W. Musselman (New York: Association Press, 1963) $7.95. An omnibus resource book for ages 5-12 years.

Camping with Retarded Persons edited by LaDonna Bogardus (9523-BC) (Nashville: General Board of Education of The United Methodist Church, 1970) Paper, $1.10. Focuses primarily on information needed by group leaders, but information on administration is also included.

Good Camping for Children and Youth of Low-Income Families by Catharine V. Richards. Children's Bureau Publication No. 463-1968, 1968. Paper, 30 cents.

When Your Family Goes Camping by Ralph Bugg (3071-BC) (Nashville: General Board of Education of The Methodist Church, 1967) Paper, 75 cents. A basic manual for families who go camping on their own.

Church Family Camps and Conferences by Elizabeth and William Genne (Philadelphia: United Church Press, 1962) Paper, $1.40. A thorough administrative and program manual.

HEALTH AND SAFETY

The Camp Nurse. Health and Safety Committee, American Camping Association, 1956. Paper, 50 cents. A guide to camp nursing and the total health program.

Life Saving and Water Safety. The American Red Cross. Paper, 75 cents. A recognized text for camp planners and administrators.

ECOLOGY, CONSERVATION, AND STEWARDSHIP

The Web of Life by John H. Storer. (New York: New American Library, Inc., 1966) Paper, 95 cents. A first book of ecology; presents in easily readable form the story of the interrelationship of all living things.

Understanding Ecology by Elizabeth T. Billington (New York: Frederick Warne & Co., 1968) $3.95. For use by junior high up.

Nature in the City by John Rublowsky (New York: Basic Books, Inc., 1967) $5.95. Science and Discovery Series.

Conservation. Camp Fire Girls, Inc., 16 East 48th Street, New York, N. Y. 10017. 75 cents. Nearly two hundred activities and projects dealing with conservation and ecology, each with a stated purpose, site, and suggested procedure.

AUDIO VISUALS

Day Camping for Your Church. 35mm, 47-frame color filmstrip with script. $7.50. Order from Cokesbury Bookstores.

Audubon Ecology Chart. (33" x 50".) National Audubon Society, 1130 Fifth Avenue, New York, N. Y. 10028. $2.15.

RESOURCES FOR CHRISTIAN OUTDOOR EDUCATION
Cooperatively Planned Materials
Outdoor Living by LaDonna Bogardus (Nashville: Abingdon Press, 1971) Comprehensive program guidance for day camp, resident camp, and other outdoor activities of the church for older elementary boys and girls.

Leader's Guide contains resources needed by each adult for advance preparation. Each, $1.50.

Packet 1 contains poems, scripture references, worship and discussion ideas, games, hymns, and songs. One needed for each adult leader. Each, $1.25.

Packet 2 has directions for use of tools, firebuilding, lashing, development of the small camp, cooking, recipes, and craft activities. At least two needed for each group. Each $1.25.

Packet 3 includes twelve discovery guides for individual use by campers in exploring, experimenting, and thinking about meanings in a specific area. One needed for every two or three campers. Each, $1.25.

Denominational Materials
(See *Church Camping* by Robert Pickens Davis for a comprehensive listing of church camping resources available from denominations.)